What GOES Around COMES Around

What GOES Around COMES Around

by: DAISY de Villeneuve

CHRONICLE BOOKS

SAN FRANCISCO

First published in the United States in 2005 by Chronicle Books LLC.

Conceived, created, and designed by Daisy de Villeneuve and Pocko Editions Ltd.
P.O. Box 20190, London, England W10 5LA

Library of Congress Cataloging-in-Publication Data available.
ISBN: 0-8118-4724-1

Manufactured in China

Edited by Nicola Schwartz
Design by Olga Norman
Cover design by Jay Salvas

Distributed in Canada by Raincoast Books
9050 Shaughnessy Street
Vancouver, British Columbia V6P 6E5

10 9 8 7 6 5 4 3 2 1

Chronicle Books LLC
85 Second Street
San Francisco, California 94105
www.chroniclebooks.com

Introduction

Dear Reader,

What Goes Around Comes Around, is a
series of portraits and stories about
encounters with girls I've known. What
these girls share in common is that they
are all the same type: bitch. I swear I
don't seek them out but they always end
up entangled in my life anyway, acting
sweet but treating me badly. They act like
we're best friends but they show up at the
wrong time, they're rude to my true
friends, they steal my men, they take what-
ever they can from me. And in the end,
they manage to somehow turn everything
around and make me feel guilty.

You know the kind of girl I'm talking about.
Why does she keep coming around?

Daisy de Villeneuve

You know who she is.

She somehow gets your telephone number and starts
calling non-stop, especially
at the wrong time. There's
always a drama, she doesn't
quite comprehend that not
only is she a total maniac,
but that maybe you have
things to do other than
listen to her whiny voice.

She's not someone you
search out, you just stumble
across her. She's normally
a friend of a friend, or
you work with her, or went
to school with her, or
she's a friend of the
family or you live with
her, or god forbid she's
a relative. It's not like
there's an out. It's kind
of about the circumstances
you encounter.

She's always asking a
million questions; Where
are you going? What are you
doing? Who invited you? Why
did they invite you? Who's

going to be there? Maybe
you'll meet someone? Do
you think He's going to be
there? What are you going
to wear? What time do you
have to be there? Do you
think there'll be food
there? What do you think
you'll have to drink?
Maybe you'll go home with
someone? Do you think you'll
go home with someone? I
bet you do go home with
someone!
   Oh, you're so lucky
you're going out and you're
gonna meet the one.

Wish I was you.

~~She~~ She tracked me down at work, I didn't even like this person, why was she calling me? Can't she sense that I don't like her? Doesn't she realise that I think she's a ✳ clingy wet-drip. Back off!

Thing~~s~~
pick ~~~~
clean
~~tavn~~

I hadn't seen her in two yea
years. I had been living
abroad. She would wri write
to me every few months. I
wasn't planning on seeing
her, but she called me and
we were in the same city. I
decided to see her, as it
had been a couple of years,
thinking that maybe she had
changed. When I met up with
her she did seem quite
mature, sk so I kind ed of
brushed the past aside and
started spending time with
her. Big mistake!

She mentioned how her friend
had slept with him, which
happened to coincide with
when I had slept with him.
She told me this information
a year after ~~thw~~ the event.
I wondered why she told me
this as she knew I had slept
with him and, if it was true
that her friend had as well
during the same time, why
was she telling me? It wasn't
like I was involved with him.
It was like some exclusive
 gossip that only she knew
about. Also, why tell me a
year later? Uh, what was the
point? You can be discreet
about these things and if
she hadn't mentioned it I
wouldn't have known. Even
though it had ~~beeb~~ been
a while, a year, it really
didn't make me feel great
to hear this.

One te time she came over to
my house and within minutes
she was trying on my shoes,
looking through my clothes
and using my make up. Plus
she wanted to borrow money.

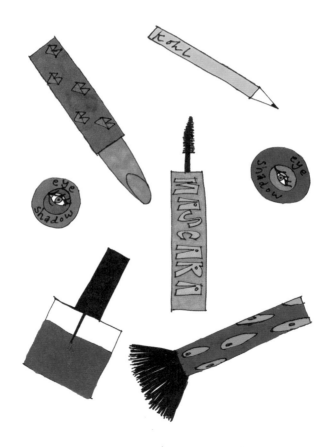

I asked her if she knew him.
I thought she probably would
know him, as they had a mutual
friend in common. I told her
I had been going out with him
for a couple months. She
responded with, "Are you sure?

I'm really good friends with
him and he's never mentioned
a girl or girlfriend". I
must have sounded quite shock-
ed at this information, as
she started to back track
saying that she wasn't
actually that good friends
with him.

She was completely annoying,
getting on my nerves,
complaining and whining.

She was sucking all the ~~ener~~
energy out from me. I end
up thinking that I should

be nice to her. She's like
a pest. I find her selfish
and the only reason she

attempts at a friendship

with me is because she
wants something.

I observed how guys would
act ari around her, the more
badly behaved she was the
more they liked her. She
could be a total bitch to
her girl friends right in
front of any man and he
would still think she was
the sweetest thing on earth.
Wearing her big fake Fendi
 sunglasses she'd say in a
baby voice, "I don't have
any money for the train",
and he would reach into
his pocket and give her
some cash.

We met up for tea. She starts
bragging to me about how she
slept with this guy that she
knew I really fancied. I

thought if I had slept with
someone that she really
fancied, she'd be the last
person I'd tell.

" You have to meet this guy,
you'll really like him," she
says. I meet him and think
he's cute, we all go back to
his house. She's running
around the house with a
camera. I'm lying on the
guy's bed with him. She
looks through the door and

goes "Oooeoooohhhhhh".

Something happens and he

gets up, she corners him
and he spends the rest of
the night with her. I leave
early in the morning. I
ask her if she slept with
him? She says "No comment".

She phoned me up and started
talking about her, eb even
knowing that she was a good
friend of mine said, ' I
really don't like that girl'.

When I walked into the room
she was wearing jeans like
mine and had done her eye-

liner like how I do mine.

Freaky Friday, I knew I

shouldn't have told her
where I bought my clothes.

The guy that I had been
seeing she was now dating.
It bothered me so much, her
subtle way of telling me how
great things were between
them. I guess what really
pissed me off was that she
was still in my life. Even
when she was 3,000 miles
awag away. She had to
creep back in! Whenever
she called me she was like,
"hiiiiii".

I first met her for like
five minutes at a trendy shop
opening. When I met her this
time she was super friendly
verging on totally fake,
acting like my new best
friend. I later found out
that she had bitched about
me to a bunch of people,
including an old friend
(he was the one that told
me), but he ~~f~~ didn't tell
me absolutely everything
she had said so as to not
upset me. But what he did
tell me I believed. I
~~belieb-belived-him-because~~
believed him because when
she did talk to me for
those five minutes when we
first met she bitched about
other people I knew, and
some I didn't know but had
heard of. She badmouthed
them terribly.
 As for what I thought of
her, well, I think she's
too fat to wear midriff
tops but I'm keeping my
opinions to myself.
 What goes around comes
around.

She phoned me up to tell me
that she had bumped into him
in the street. According to

her, he had asked about me
and mentioned he'd like to
see me. Apparently he ~~said~~
asked her if he should call
me? She told him not to
bother calling me. She knew

perfectly well that I wanted
to see him.

I felt guilty for not liking
her. I was wanted to kill the
person that had given her my
telephone number. She called
me up and asked if I wanted
to go get some dinner. I
felt sorry for her and,
unfortunately, agreed to
join her for food, thinking
maybe she's okay; it's only
that I get that kind of a
needy vibe from her. Over
dinner she complained
about her love life. I
must have been bored and I
told her too much about
mine, so after that she'd
call sporadically,ranting
on about her "I HATE MEN"
attitude and feeling that
we were united in having
something in common, except
she had projected that onto
me. I never said I shared
her opinions. I needed to
get as far away from her
as possible.

She once phoned me up while
I was living in Paris, to
ask if she could come stay
with me and bring her cat. I
lived alone and I didn't
want her or her cat to
bombard me. From that telephone converstation her
last words were, "will you
support me?" I wasn't sure
if she meant emotionally
or financially. With her
wild child antics, I just
didn't want to know.

She calls about Ipm and
he's still in my bed. She
says to me, "Did you kiss
him?" "Yes" I reply. "What
else?" she says "You know.."
I say. "Is he there?" she
says. "Yes" I say. "How
could you! I liked him"
(this is coming from someone that has a boyfriend).
Anyway you couldn't have
had sex with him because
you have your period. I'm
putting the phone down".
she says.

We go out for drinks and she
proceeds to tell me that she
doesn't think he's for me,
that he probably won't call
me and that she can't see
the appeal.

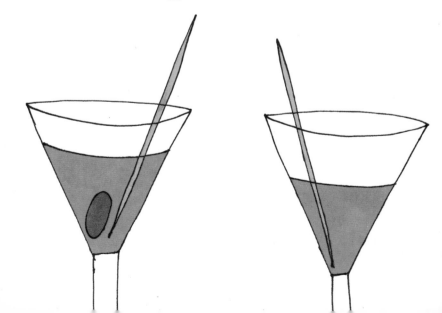

he'll find your weak spots
nd start digging.

Her make-up was all messed up,
it kept getting in her eyes.
"Don't rub your eyes" I said.
Once we were outside and had
walked ten minutes, she
would turn to me and say, "I
need to re-do my make-up".
After three attempts of her
coming and going back to the
house.I should have figured,
if this was annoying at the
beginning... just imagine
how the evening would end!

One time she was at my house
and we were talking about
this guy that we both knew,
than all of a sudden she's
like, "my friend's going
out with him". I had been
seeing him too but he had

been in New York for a

couple months; I had to hold

back my tears. When I

confronted him he said,
"yes, I do have a new girl-

friend". Then said- he said

in regard to us, "we weren't
really a couple. We were
just friends that had sex".

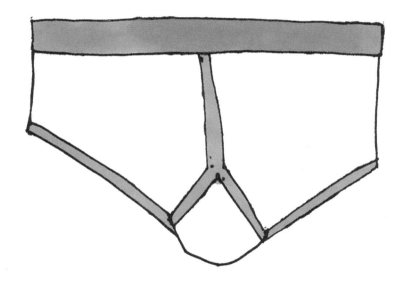

One day I went over to her
house and she didn't say
that much. She stormed out,
I asked her boyfriend, "
"what's wrong with her?"
"She thinks you're being a
bitch" he said. "Why?" I
said. "I don't know, You
ask her?" he said. I
called her when I got
home. Her boyfriend answered, "Can I speak to her?"
I said. "She doesn't want
to talk to you" he said.
"Why?" I said. "she thinks
you're being a bitch".
"Why does she think I'm
being a bitch? What did I
do?" I said. "Ask her" he
said. "How can I ask her if
she doesn't want to talk to
me?" I said. I called back
the next day, the boyfriend
answered, same reply.

She'll call and I'll d̶ say
that ±8- I'm in a meeting
or really busy. "Can I call
you back?" I'm trying to get
out of talking to her. I am
truly busy but I'm reminded
of the excuses guys use on
me all the time like the all
too familiar one, "I'll call
you later!" When they never
call, I end up not making
any plans with people just
in case they ¥ call, but
they don't and I end up
getting totally stressed
out. So I k̶e̶ keep this in
mind and tell myself I'll
call her back in a few days.

I caught them kissing in
the toilets, my best friend
and my date.

She ~~had~~ has a heart of steel.

completely no sense of other
peoples feelings.

I tell her that I'm sensitive
and she says, "I'm sensitive.
I'm sensitive.I'm sensitive.
Get over it. Pull your socks
up".

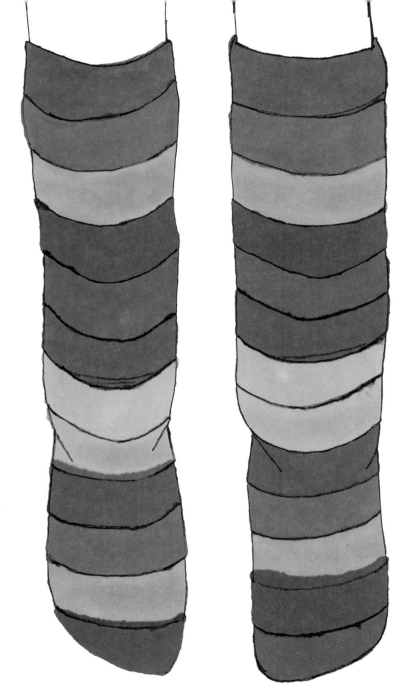

When I saw her I noticed that
her lipstick was all smudged.
She asked if she could borrow
mine to re-apply.

I think she's been taking
Stupid pills again.

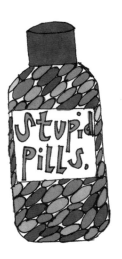

Y ou wouldn't think that
your so called best friend
who is married with a child
would pounce on the guy that
you've been sleeping with,
then state that it was okay
'coz "you weren't together".

At the moment she doesn't
pick up the phone when I
call 'coz she has caller ID,
sees my name and doesn't
want to answer. She owes me
money and can't deal with
responsibility.

She gives me a permanent
anxiety attack.

What really bugged me about
her was that whenever she
was over at my house she
would rummage through my

medicine cabinet and use
all my beauty products.
Especially my expensive

moisturising creams that

I'd purchased at Fred Segals

in L.A.

Or maybe it was that she'd
squeeze into one of my old
dresses and say that she
'had ⱬ to wear it' to the
wedding she was attending
as 'it e would be perfect'!
Funny how she seemed to be
that little bit bigger than
me (2 dress sizes). She
returned the dress but
failed to mention that
she had ripped it while
out and about. I could see
that it had been torn
from the invisible thread
that was holding it
together.

Rarely do I freak out, but
one time I do. I tell her
that I don't want to see
her again and 'not to call
me', because she's so ~~inte~~
intense, such a nuisance,
busybody, pest, weirdo,
insane, annoying and utterly
crazy. She calls regardless.
I am completely sincere
when I say I can't deal
with her. What part of that
does she not understand?

I told her that my date had
stood me up. She said, 'well
obviously he got a better
offer!'

I ded- decided to bring a new
friend to lunch with me, someone my old girl friend hadn't
met before (and not knowing
her step-mother would be there).
During li lunch my old friend
turned to me and said, "Who

is this obnoxious girl you
brought along?"

Her goody two shoes routine

~~mad~~ makes me sick.

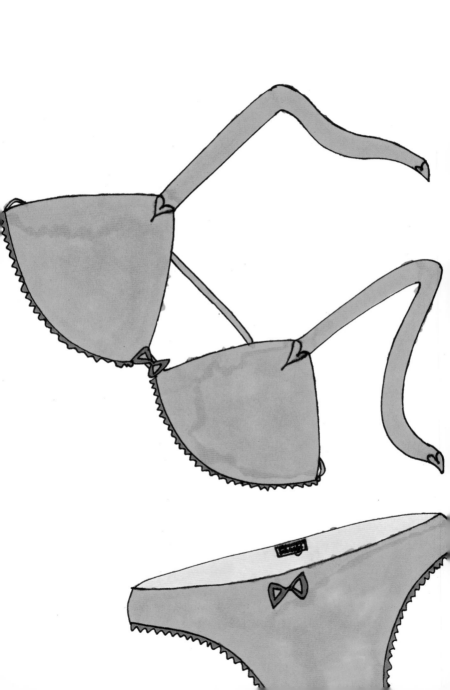

When we meet up she tells
me that she got together
with him. In a very blasé
tone she says, "he told me
he didn't want to be with
you".

Memo:

January 1st

New Year's Resolution

I need to leave out all destructive people from my life. I know who they are and I need to stop spending time with them. I always feel so guilty, but I shouldn't. I can't be friends with everyone! I'm so over so many people that I don't need to waste my time anymore. I can't be friends with someone who doesn't respect me, even if they say they do. I want someon to appreciate me, not be condesc ending towards me which I fe constantly.

I decide ~~r~~ to take some action
and go see Dr.Stein, a

therapist.

$ I5θ later and he hadn't
really told me anything I
didn't already know...
"If you feel their energy
is negative, it may help
to edit some people out
of your life; with others
it's not so easy as you
have a history with them.

People can bring good and
bad feelings into one's
life," he said.

TELEPHONE
NUMBERS
&
ADDRESSES

A
B
C
D
E
F
G
H
I
J
K
L
M
N
O
P
Q
R
S
T
U
V
W
X
Y
Z

Notes
Don't fo
Satu

1
2
3
4
5
6
7
9
0

REDIAL

Sometimes I think that I
should change my telephone
number. But why? She would
just be able to find the
new number from someone
else! Plus I'd have to
give everyone my new
number and that would be
such a bore. Maybe I should
block her number next time
she ~eak~ calls, with any
~li~ luck she may get the
hint?

She called me and said,'I'm
not supposed to tell you this
but I thought you should know
that 1 think he's going out
with her and apparently he's

stayed at her house everyday

this week.' In this really
condescending voice she kept
saying, "Are you depressed?"

She should think before she
speaks!

When I last saw her she was
like, "I love you", as if
that term of endearment is
supposed to she change
everything. Like I'm going
to forgive her. I don't
think she even realises
she's done anything wrong.

the
end

The Author

Born in 1975 and conceived to the pop song "Kung Fu Fighting," Daisy de Villeneuve was brought up in the world of fashion: her mother, Jan, is a model and her father, Justin, is a photographer. Her illustrations have appeared everywhere from shoe boxes and fashion ads to her own line of housewares. She exhibits internationally and lives in London. Her first book, *He Said, She Said*, illustrates snippets of stolen conversations between men and women. *What Goes Around Comes Around* is her second book.

The Typewriter

The text of this book was written with a second-hand Olympia, model number 784345, made in 1947 and bought by the author at Squires' Antiques in Kent 56 years later. The original advertisment assured us that this typewriter was "the next generation of quality and precision."